CONSUMED

For Nancy

Glad you came to the
reading tonight!

David Hng

CONSUMED

Poems by David Hill

K EN A RNOLD B OOKS LLC
Portland, Oregon

Some of the poems in this book previously appeared in the following media:

US magazines: *Gargoyle, Troubadour.*
UK magazines: *Candelabrum, Envoi, Exile, First Time, Iota, Lateral Moves,
The New Writer, Outposts, Peer Poetry International, Poetic Licence, Poetry
News, Rustic Rub, Weyfarers.*
Other magazines: *Edizioni Universum Newsletter* (Italy), *Metverse Muse*
(India), *Page Eighty Four* (Belgium), *Pilvax* (Hungary).
Online products: *Journalism Online* (India), *Patchword* (Spain),
Underground Window (US).
Anthologies: *Dialogue Through Poetry* (Rattapallax Press, US), *Disasters in the
Kitchen* (Wendy Webb Books, UK), *Future Welcome* (DC Books, Canada), *The
Poetic Principle* (Mind Print, Hungary), *Poetry as a Foreign Language* (White
Adder Press, UK), *The Sonnet at the Millennium* (Open University Shakespeare
Society, UK).
Broadcast: *Tilos Radio* (Hungary), Danish national radio.

Library of Congress Control Number: 2008927445

Published by KenArnoldBooks, LLC,
1330 SW 3rd Avenue, 810, Portland, OR 97201

ISBN: 978-0-9799634-6-9

www.kenarnoldbooks.com

VI

Contents

Entry Visa

The word for yes is "Ah, no."
Truckers able to curse in four human languages
Will give you a ride to the border.
You will stay in hotels where the red tap doesn't work
And the blue tap delivers hot water.
Forgotten towns will hoist blackened apartment blocks
Against snowy mountains.
The sky is usually yellow.
Sometimes a baroque church will surprise you,
But usually it's the chickens, the mud tracks,
Buses puffing, pulling in where
You could not imagine its being anyone's stop,
That will get to you.
Castles will rise out of nowhere,
Lit up at night.
Do not ski
Or invest.
Ride the hearts of the combs of hills.
Stay as long as you like.

Physiognomy

I find myself forgetting what you look like
Whenever I've not seen you for a day.
You go all one-dimensional and book-like.
Your living essence somehow slips away.

I try to picture your complete ensemble,
Or visualize some individual part.
I end up with this strange amorphous womble,
Or else I simply don't know where to start.

I can't explain the overarching point of you,
I can't describe what makes you so unique;
Why every single muscle, bone and joint of you
Can make my physiognomy go weak.

But when you're here, the whole of you, in focus,
And do that look that means you want a kiss—
Ker-pow! Abracadabra! Hocus pocus!
No images, no explanations. This.

Silly Dog

I prefer to remember
My first impressions of you
When you followed me and my friend
For about half an hour,
Bounding around us,
Tail hyperactive and tongue out,
Twisting your head and rolling your eyes
Just to make it that little bit more obvious
That you wanted to play;

And later that day when I watched you
Chase after every horse and cart,
Darting in front of the horse and barking madly,
And follow every human
Backwards and forwards along the village's one road,
Always to get shooed away,
And the way all the other dogs
Snarled and shouted at you when they saw you.
Then I realized
That most animals didn't like you
For the same reason that I did.
Because you're a silly dog.

I prefer not to remember
A few days later
When I bent down to stroke you
And my guitar case slipped from my shoulder
And hit your soft side
And you sprang away
And wouldn't come back.
And afterwards, whenever you passed me
While following other humans
Backwards and forwards,
You looked at me with hurt in your yellow eyes
And looked away again.
But those other humans
Didn't want to play with you
And I did,
You silly dog.

The Eighties Better World Makers

The style looks quaint now, but at least we had one.
We strove to serve the fans, not cause them strain.
A pinstriped too-big jacket, or a plaid one,
Conveyed that we were there to entertain.
Out went the backwards glamor of the pauper;
We taught the era's youth: look up, not down.
The high priestess of fun was Cyndi Lauper,
And Woodstock was the bird from Charlie Brown.
Our politics were simple but constructive:
Madonna made materialists seductive;
The Berlin Wall fell down when Elton blew.
We knew what friends were for; we saw through phonies.
We made, but now disown, the Bills and Tonys.
Tonight thank God it's them instead of you.
As flies swarmed round an Ethiopian face,
A Collins fill coaxed Taylor's restless bass.

Law Break Girl

She grabbed my legs while I was swimming in the sea—
Perhaps her way of showing her affection.
She said she was the diver and the reef was me.
I didn't really follow the connection.

Her hair was spiky and her fingernails were black.
Two-thirds my height, and coveted the *whole* me.
She said she'd kill me if I didn't kiss her back.
She said she'd strangle any girl that stole me.

From beach to pickup and to seven dizzy weeks
And then the night the law men came and cuffed her.
She broke and entered, I suppose there were some leaks.
And pretty soon I realized that I luffed her.

Her dried deodorant, her birthmarks and her bust
Disturb me when I'm delicately sleeping.
But safe and sound from raging arguments or lust
Now that I'm certain she won't catch me peeping.

She grabbed my legs while I was swimming in the sea—
Perhaps her way of showing her affection.
She said she was the diver and the reef was me.
I didn't really follow the connection.

Thunder

Past midnight, and the thunder comes unbeckoned,
Persuades the rain and dissipates the heat,
Flicks on my light for half a ghostly second
And triggers off alarms across the street.

And lying here, I think of how you'd wake me
When thunder came, how sweetly you'd move in
For the unspoken hug, the way you'd take me
And tame your prickling skin against my skin;

And how I'd try my hardest to console you,
And whisper it was OK, I was here.
A spark across the solitude that stole you.
The thunder's gone now. All that's left is fear.

Vârcolac

I do find Transylvania congenial:
Haunting a forest or a Saxon town.
The tourists love me, but it's all quite menial.
Moldavia was where I wore the crown.

A corner of first Rome's then Kiev's empire,
I stood for all things Caesar never tames.
Werewolf, vermicolacius, or vampire:
My legend, like my towns, had many names.

Hero of global culture, I grew slicker,
Perfected chilling smiles and licked my lips.
But long before fresh blood became my liquor,
I ate the sun and moon. I was eclipse.

Between the mouths of Dnister and of Duna
Is still where I return to rear my young.
I teach them *somnul dulce, noapte bună*:
Our vowel-rich Thraco-Latin mother-tongue.

Olympian

You'll hear a lot of tales. My brandy costs three grand
A bottle. I got rich on fraud and contraband.
I've written off two dozen bikes with my sheer size.
I pinned a charging bull to the black earth in mid-
Conversation. I dreamed of boxing as a kid
But got the taste for weights from giving piggy rides
To my eccentric coach. Want to hear one that's true?
I cheated the world champion (my compatriot, too)
Out of a gold he could have got. I feigned complete
Exhaustion while he chose his final weight. He beat
The rest, but I came back to pip him by a pound.
That earned me a Red Star! Who says the Communists
Didn't reward initiative? These things astound
The students at my business school, receptionists

At my eight firms—they can't believe that I was proud
To represent the Union, when these days I'm so
"Entrepreneurial." They wonder, furrow-browed,
About "justice," about "the system." All I know
Is how to leave excessive scoops of powdered chalk
Dancing the dais; to do the forward-backward walk
As knees and elbows jackknife in a taut relief:
My shoulder-blades kneading the cheers, the self-belief,
The notoriety, into self-selling sheen.
I only wish those tales were even more far-fetched.
Here's me, badly-defined bulk that I was, in stretched
Red top, hammer and sickle ironed on between
My tits. Kissing my gold. My old Olympian fame.
You weren't yet born, but you're nostalgic all the same.

The Future

As I remember it, the future
Was always about distances.
How we would cover them, physically,
Riding from street to street, city to city, planet to planet,
With our rockets, rocket-propelled cars, and jetpacks,
Or simply standing still on moving pavements,
Resting our hefty leather briefcases beside us,
Checking our lipstick in compact mirrors.

And then the emotional distances:
The cold logic and scientific expertise
With which we would analyze our predicaments,
Lay out our plans of action.
Never avoiding warp factor nine
Out of an irrational aversion to that number.
Invariably planning our ingestion and exercise
In strict adherence to our bodily needs.

How silly we were
In those days, before we were born!
Look what's actually happened.
Instead of finding new ways to cover large spaces,
We pretend to have made the spaces smaller
With communication tools.
And what a ridiculous idea

That everyone would understand all the technology!
Had we forgotten the division of labor,
And didn't we realize the divisions would become
More and more multi-cellular?
To think we would have become smarter—
How stupid!

And
(As I wait for you
To return my messages
Through any or all of these
Non-threatening gadgets
With which I have tried to reach you all day)
Did we really ever imagine
That it wouldn't end up being
Distance
That would defeat understanding
And reason,
Distance
That would cover us?

Hard to Get

Last night you offered me your love,
Under the influence of drink.
I didn't take you straight away;
I had to have a little think.

I thought about it long and hard:
I think I'd like you to be mine.
And now I really must insist
You have another glass of wine.

Ended

It's better if I stay away.
She could be anywhere. She may
Be praying that I won't come any more.
And there's no guarantee I'd say
The things I didn't say before:
That we were two sides of a single door.
That I was night and she was day
And vice versa, either or,
Forever changing, always two but one.
No sooner ended than begun.

It's better if he comes today.
At least I won't know what to say.
I may say the wrong thing. I did before,
And closed the door and opened up the way,
And turned it into either or.
We were the one thing I was praying for,
October spring, and fall in May,
The ceiling and the upstairs floor,
A constant contradiction, one but two.
Come here, let's stop and start anew.

Last Love

His voice sounds different on the phone.
The public pose: the man bereaved.
But over red clandestine wine,
The widower, the divorcee,
Dissolve to him and nervous me
And what, time willing, still might be.
His patronizing kids and mine
Say: it's so nice you're not alone.
Who is deceiving, who deceived?

He's quite convinced she waits above
But wouldn't grudge him this late thrill.
We book a genteel package flight—
A dream vacation!—But he broods,
Picks over unaccustomed foods,
And will not guide me through his moods.
I hang on to his arm, last night,
Last act that might betoken love,
And—touching up my rouge—last will.

On Your Wedding

And so, in this public yet private maneuver,
With signing of forms and with kisses,
You pledge to show everyone—friend or reprover—
And not least, each other—what bliss is;
Face bureaucrats, God and the salesman from Hoover
As mister and missus.

And so, in accord with the prescripts of gender,
Which secretly, softly propel us,
You make one from two, and immediately render
The rest of us fair maids and fellas
Ecstatic and proud for you, tearful and tender,
And seethingly jealous.

Bachelor Meal

The bacon and the bread are both inspected,
And any bits with fungus on, rejected.
The uninfested pieces are then fried,
And served with button mushrooms on the side.

Pavarotti's Lament

Today I thought I'd do a bit of dusting
And clean the three big armchairs in the lounge.
The way that those two leave things, it's disgusting.
It's Pavarotti scrubs, while they just scrounge.

Now, I don't mean to carp about Carreras,
But while I'm touching up the pinewood glaze,
He's sat out swatting insects on the terrace—
The only Bs he ever hits, these days.

Who cleaned up last? It must have been Domingo.
What that guy's hidden, no one else can find.
It's not as if he's talented. He's Ringo,
While I, of course, am John and Paul combined.

Oh sure, we've had a few good games of Twister,
That time we all went surfing was a scream.
Just wish I could work out which ugly sister
Keeps hogging all the blankets while I dream.

Global Village Idiot

I was born in lovely North America,
And I grew up tall and strong there.
But like most folks up in North America,
I always knew I didn't belong there.
Well, they sometimes say America's a melting pot,
But that just isn't so,
Cause everybody knows what kind of blood they've got,
And wants everyone they know, to know.

As for me,
I was proud to have my roots deep in a continent that starts and
    ends with E;
Lapsed RC,
With a love of complex novels and a healthy disregard for MTV.
And depressed by the consumerist society
Of malls,
Hard sells and cold calls,
With a Kafkaesque gloom I'd retreat to my room,
Sticking existential poems on my walls.

Oh, greed is bad and suffering is noble;
I longed to leave the rat race and go global!

So I moved to my ancestral heartland,
With a thirst for music, painting, sculpture—
Found I understood the arts of my heartland,
But I never really got ... the culture.
I'd be arguing in English with some friend of mine,
Who was usually a dumb ex-pat,
And the folks would glare at me like I'm some foreign swine—
Well, I ask you, imagine that!

So I cried
For this customer-unfriendly and neurotic little land to come on side
For a wide-
Spread acceptance of the liberal and democratic views I held
   with pride.
I was heard by a discriminating audience
Of one—
My local-born son—
Who said: "Go home Dad, and if you still feel sad,
Get yourself a nice motel room and a gun."

Oh how was I to know this thing would snowball?
I've got no home, my soul is lost, it's—global!

Then I bumped my head and dozed off for a century
And I woke up really bright and breezy,
And I found that in the twenty-second century
They were taking the whole nation thing easy.
The concept of a country as no more than a space
Made every sword a plow,
And instead of the long history of their own race,
Kids were taught about the whole world: now.

Playground names
Were not thrown by politicians in a petty war of territorial claims;
Up in flames
Went all separatist agendas—to reach out and understand
    were now the aims.
And of course there was a single common language,
But, Mensch,
The language was French,
Which to me is pure sound, so I just went to ground,
And I dug myself a lonely little trench.

What use to me a modem or a mobile?
Oh spare the village fool: world, don't go global!

Where No One Mows Lawns

In a city where no one mows lawns,
Where the very idea is upsetting,
You're disturbed by the hot April dawns
And the grass and the beech trees erupting.

And we're wearing our black hair and jeans,
And we're back in Kentucky Fried Chicken,
And the streets are an orgy of greens,
And the beats of our metal riffs darken,

And a woman and man, hand-in-hand,
Stride in and they peer in a corner,
And they turn and, as if it were planned,
They stride out, in a single maneuver;

And the clouds and the perfumey breeze
Are delivering hot April showers
From beyond the black mushrooms of trees
In a city where no one owns mowers.

Ludwigsburg Love Song

Thick vine leaves, blue-green, crisp on biting, bitter,
In fields that nudge the Schwarzwald's outer glades,
Beneath the Hilltop castle's distant glitter;
Grow bristly: weave your tightened knotted thread
Across proud domes: become the taut black braids
That clamber my Karibik girl's strong head.

Warm church bells in your warped wood tower, pressing
An ancient freshness through the gold air's gauze,
Bach-harmonizing God's-love's-nature's laws:
Toll, toll: be my Karibik girl's calm tones;
The vigor of her old-young voice, caressing,
Which beckons, chides, embraces and condones.

Though kings of Württemberg to their fine gardens
Once brought bright cacti; shipped flamingos in;
Enjoyed their noon-time strolls beneath the fronds
Of palm trees; still, I beg their gracious pardons:
I'll choose my night-dark love, our home-grown bonds,
Her church bell curves, her tough smooth vine leaf skin.

Loneliness Bridge

If you stand at the tip of the island, with the river pouring by,
And the city rollicking either side until it becomes the sky,
When the pick of the buildings are floodlit and the purple
    horizon is dry,
If you count the bridges one by one you'll possibly catch my eye.

And the first bridge down is the Chain Bridge, geometrical and clean,
And the second bridge down is Elizabeth Bridge, named after
    the beautiful queen,
And the third bridge down is the Freedom Bridge with its girders
    painted green,
But the fourth bridge down is Loneliness Bridge, and that's
    where I'm frequently seen.

If you're breakfasting at the Angelika, with the river funneling past,
Its memoried water like elephants' skin, its optimist fishers miscast,
And the Fabergé egg of the Parliament a messageless radio mast,
A signal of love might reach me yet, before I gulp my last.

And the first bridge down is the Chain Bridge, mechanical and neat,
And the second bridge down is Elizabeth Bridge, her petticoats
    lapping her feet,
And the third bridge down is the Freedom Bridge, and I hope
    you'll be free, my sweet,
Cause the fourth bridge down is Loneliness Bridge: that's where
    I suggest that we meet.

Car

They're almost to the car
By the time Julie makes the introductions:
"My old friend Sue Wright,
My boyfriend Stephen Whistler."

"Do you smoke, Whistle?"
Asks the blond ponytail, the white T-shirt.
"Ah, no, no, I don't actually, thanks,"
Says he, thickset, too serious.

Later, while Julie's driving, chatting,
With the other two in the back,
Sue spots a piece of orange pulp
In a corner of Julie's wide smile.

"Someone hasn't finished all her food," Sue laughs,
Hooking it out with a firm fingernail.
And: "Want some orange?"—
She jocularly offers it to Stephen;

Who, before anyone knows what's happening,
Takes the whole finger into his mouth
And sucks.

Naturally

No need to use protection, she insists.
They're naturally insured against all risk
By like-mindedness, two clean bills of health
And the stark geometry of the lunar month.

But then, a hold-up. She's broken down in sobs.
(Because I bring her so much joy, he hopes.)
"I'll stop soon," she sighs. "What—stop our affair?
Is that the matter?" "No! Stop shedding tears

Over *him*." The aloof man who's had her crying,
Writing long letters, eight months unrequited.
An emotional membrane, keeping their sex
Naturally insured. Free from all risk.

Glue

They met again by accident, just days
After they'd finished doing their exams,
And muttered some embarrassed epigrams
While trying to avoid each other's gaze.

"Hi there!" she said. Said he: "Hi! How are you?"
She pondered for a while, then told him: "Great!"
And this reply seemed so appropriate
She subsequently stuck to it like glue.

"How's everything?" "Um ... great!" "Nice weather!" "Oh,
It's great!" And when he asked, "How did they go,
Those tough exams we worked for all those years?"

And she responded, with no variation,
"Oh, great!"—this was the final confirmation
Of his suspicions and of her worst fears.

Love at the Poetry Reading

Among the screaming crowds at my recital,
She sat there, awestruck, drinking every line.
A common girl, I guessed, no noble title,
Perhaps not rich or clever—still, looked fine.
Then, at the end, a-quake with trepidation,
She tiptoed up to take a closer look;
And, too enthralled to start a conversation,
She shyly smiled—and then—she bought my book!

Romantic odes and matrimonial idylls
Began to form within my fertile brain;
And though this stranger did present some riddles,
Just one bright thought consigned them to the drain.
Who cares if she's had proletarian lovers,
Or if she buys her dresses off the hook?
Provided she's not dull between the covers.
But then, how could she be? She bought my book!

Yes, for her sheer good taste I'd gladly pardon
Her many faults, whatever they may be.
She might not have a golf course in her garden,
Nor drive a fast Ferrari—fine by me!
It's OK if her conversation bores me;
I don't mind if she's not a gourmet cook;
As long as she just slavishly adores me—
Which, obviously, she does. She bought my book!

Ex Directory

My telephone rang, and when I answered it, a woman's voice asked whether I was a certain company—the company, in fact, that was a former employer of my ex-girlfriend. I told the woman no, and started to add that I probably could help her find what she was looking for, but she interrupted me, apologizing for dialing the wrong number, and hastily put down the receiver.

Twenty minutes later the phone rang again. It was the same woman with the same question, but this time I recognized her voice. She was a former colleague of mine at a company where I no longer worked. I greeted her by name and told her who I was, at which point she became even more apologetic and less open to my offers of help. She quickly rang off.

After a few minutes' reflection, I remembered that an ex-colleague of my ex-girlfriend, who was also an ex-tenant of my flat, had applied for a job with my ex-employer. Perhaps, I surmised, her application had mentioned my phone number, which my ex-colleague, wishing to discuss the application, had taken to be the applicant's work number. Not knowing that I knew about my ex-girlfriend's ex-colleague's job application, I deduced, my own ex-colleague was embarrassed to find herself talking to a stranger on what she took to be the wrong number—all the more so after discovering that this stranger was, in fact, somebody she knew.

Trying to be helpful and at the same time discreet, I looked up the phone number of my one-time paramour's erstwhile place of employ and telephoned my own previous treadmill, intending to tell my old workmate the number she required and then terminate the conversation with no further small talk. However, when I called the enterprise I once served and asked to speak to my former sister-in-servitude, I was told that she no longer worked there.

I returned to my sunny balcony and my book.

Moneytime

One kopeck: George cocksure, his sleek lance drilling
The writhing dragon's jaws, a mint-clean slaughter.
Another George who trusts in God: one quarter.
Then three top-heavy, spindly blooms: a schilling.

Here's Poland: pious kings the west's forgotten.
Thick Vegas chips, a range of slogans written
Around their rims, like lolly jokes: that's Britain.
Here's France: a nymph. Uzbekistan: some cotton.

I've got all sorts here: artists, schoolbook heroes,
A few big cats, ten different types of eagle,
Outdated coats of arms (We're old! We're regal!),
Nice landscapes, names of central bank heads, zeroes.

Some people find my passion for it funny.
A world that longs for yield, allows for clearing,
Finds packages attractive, measures gearing,
And lives on credit, has no time for money.

Spinster of This Day

I've been working for the state
For two decades and a year,
Getting bus fares at half rate
And accommodation here,
In a row of thin-walled proletarian hovels,
Where I tend my skin and nails
And my independent mind—
Stepping lightly from the scales
To my tiny bedroom lined
With contemporary Anglo-Saxon novels.

My possessions, in the main,
Are in Mom and Dad's spare room.
Once a month I take the train
To be cooked for and resume
Country habits and the hard chair in the middle;
And endeavor to describe
Some great band, some actor's face,
The intoxicating vibe
Yet relaxed and steady pace
Of my urbanite, pre-menopausal idyll.

My anachronistic post
Will be scrapped when I retire,
So I come in late and coast,
Surf the internet, inquire
Into other people's wars and wealth and hunger.
I'm the spinster of this day.
Not declaiming, center-stage,
But enjoying my own play.
Would you say I look my age?
No, and neither would my man, who's twelve years
    younger.

Ditch

A ditch dig by some workmen, not filled in,
Has saved them half the trouble, has invited
Detritus from the street into its cubic meter.

Seeds, soil and twigs agreeing on a brown.
Pink meat, potato peelings, jointly stinking.
Car bumpers blanched to cardboard, overturned and bearing

Two fingers' depth of two-week-old soiled rain.
Soft newspapers talked out of their creased straightness,
Torn not like paper. Cracked white bags that once were bottles.

All kicked, shed, thrown, remain where they convene:
A place where they have no less business being
Than any other. Perfumed women walk past, talking.

Snow

We forgive you every time, snow:
We love you:
In the night-time,
Which you turn from a time
Into a small, soft and silent place,
Safe and like indoors.
We love the pastel-orange sky
Which you choose to fall from,
Flakes clear and separate all the way up.
Trees ladle you thick
Into their thin branches
To pose in you, flattered.
Men come out to spade you
From the driveways you have clogged
And are suddenly friendly.
Cars cluster under you, wear your hood,
Or lap your slush;
Statues put you on.
Dogs eat you, crazy.
Lovers breathe you.
The city turns into a little town,
The obsolete castle into a live watch-tower,
The house into a cottage.
It happens in a planetarium, and in slow-motion.
We thrill and forgive you every time.

In the morning there will be traffic-jams,
Warnings, delays, deaths of the old and the homeless,
Hooters.
In a day or two there will be pack ice,
Impossible to walk on.
But now,

Now,
A spindly tree just up the road
Has just decided to shed a shower of powder of you
Suddenly into the air, without sound;
A blackbird has created a gap
In the high, narrow, otherwise perfect crest of you
Along the second bar
Of a railing.
Stop press.
Hold the front page
And read all about it.
Those are two things
That have happened.

Butterfly

Black stockings wrinkled at the knee,
Untouchable, in laughing fits,
She hovers by a seat that's free
Adjacent to where Albert sits.

Although her boyfriend may entreat
And point towards another chair,
She laughs and hovers by the seat
Near Albert. She has long black hair.

But suddenly they notice that
The next compartment has more space.
They fly and change. The doors slam shut,
And Albert slowly lifts his face.

Analogies with butterflies
Go flitting through his dusty mind:
A clichéd image to disguise
Neglected years and hope resigned.

Twenty-four Seven

In duffel coat, green jeans and cap coquettish,
She toothily suggests a change of plan:
Before the film, indulgement of her fetish.
Her man consents. They go to see The Man.

Play, lighters! Lick the foil and make it rustle
And coax the clustering smack to gently smoke!
Close, curtains! And exclude the Camden bustle!
They gather round, except her loving bloke.

Coil, vapor! Let us wond'ringly peruse you!
Now squirt, syringe! And seek the well-used vein!
Embrace, o junkies! Let the high infuse you!
Her calm abstaining beau does not complain.

The lawyers who frequent her dungeon weekly
For water-sports, the cane, and things more vile,
Don't humor her caprices quite as meekly
As he does, for his baby squirrel's smile.

Toy Boy

I love him like a mother loves her son.
Don't let him know I said that. God forbid.
He's very sensitive, that little kid.
I'm training him, you know. I've got a plan.
He won't grow up like other men have done.
My boy will never hurt me like they did.

I love her. Making love to her is fun.
Anything that I want to do, I can.
Her bulky body's mine, her female smell
Suffuses my smooth arms. And I'm a man,
Grown-up and strong. If you'll excuse the pun,
I'd say we know each other very well.

My lovely, only one,
Nine a.m. and your sleepy flesh amid
Rough blankets on an old divan.
What have you got to sell?

A Charitable Act

Well, since you've asked,

I'm not sure if I'm doing it
Out of pure generosity of heart

Or whether I am the victim
Of emotional blackmail.

Why don't you tell me
Which would make you feel less guilty.

Then I'll know
That it's the other one.

Temptation

A man would feel temptation, yearn to sin,
If he just caught one glimpse of female skin,
Or if a girl, alone, came up to talk.
So silent, veiled, escorted we must walk.

A doctor would be tempted from his wife
If women's flesh should come beneath his knife,
And girls at work would make boys' thoughts impure.
So we must ditch career and seek no cure.

So this is Islam! Formerly we thought
The Prophet—while his wife was working—taught
Respect for people, abstinence from rage.
Now you have made our faith into a cage.

Or have you? If you dared to raise these veils
Which stop our evil charms corrupting males,
You'd find us yet more tempting than you think.
We still wear make-up: lustrous mauve, bright pink.

Feeling Horny

More than any other instrument
A French horn becomes a part of its player.
It's a long proboscis
Protruding from pursed lips
That never lose contact with it,
But open either side to breathe
Like gills.
Its great tapered coil
Is an extension of a right arm
Which by some jiggery-pokery inside the bell
Can completely alter the tone
From comforting trombone to brash bugle.
Three left-hand fingers
Meet neat valves in straight lines
Which suddenly zoom off
Into improbable loops:
A child's crazy scribblings
Or a sparkler's tracings against the sky
Described in metal piping.
The unit of horn plus player is
Something amiably strange:
A species of marine life related to the octopus,
An engine from the age of steam.

A horn player wages a constant war
Against his own saliva and condensed breath
Rusting his instrument,
Running down and wetting his sleeve.
Between movements or while playing
Or even while acknowledging applause,
A whole row of them
Will sit there
Quite happily and matter-of-factly
Tilting their horns a half or a full turn,
Or through a sort of figure of eight,
Tipping and shaking them,
Blowing into them,
Holding them aloft and sucking out of them,
Removing large or small lengths of tube
To flick out arcs of droplets,
Replacing them with a clear chink,
Tending and adjusting.
They gently remind the audience
That art is a technical affair
As well as an organic one.
Among the feelings
The music evokes in the listeners
Creep happy memories
Of good plumbers they have known.

The Second Boyfriend

She hasn't seen his body
Completely unclothed,
Isn't certain
What it will all be like,

But she imagines the silent logic,
The pretty coherence
With which the parts will present themselves,
And loves it preemptively.

Though she stammers now,
She knows that then
Things a little beyond her
Will spring to mind.

The Other Man

After our frustrating conversation—
Rare for us to catch each other in—
Still the will's there, the organized passion,
Still the times she's home and on her own
    Are times when I've got stuff on.

Coming off the phone, I boil fusilli;
Splash a few drops of sauce on my hand.
And now that tongue of mine's out, greedily
Dabbing the thumb crotch, scooping around
    The soft lips. Her blind dachshund.

The Lazy Man

The busy people bustle round her
To bestow conventional compliments
After the recital;

But he, with his huge heart in his mouth
From the beauty of the music,
When she asks if he enjoyed it,

Merely cries "oh!" and grabs her hand,
Then grows embarrassed
And excuses himself.

Laziness can be difficult to spot.
It can hide under the covers of hard work.
Its essence is introversion.

Medalist's Husband

It's like, surreal. She's climbed that hill.
How lucky can our star get?
A squashed leaf on the sidewalk till
I honed her, picked her target.

I'd love to meet a head of state,
The Pope, or Radolf Gandhi.
I play rock bass, and punctuate
Chord changes with glissandi.

Storchenbotschaft

Our names are on the headstones of our husbands,
Awaiting date of death. This warms our hearts.
Our friend's the man who makes the region's shop signs;
Our kids patrol their land in horse-drawn carts.

This spring the storks, fashionably untended,
With unkempt nests for nodding over brood,
Low-flying, halfway tame, wholly enchanted,
Did not home here. Nor did the frogs, their food.

First year I can remember when they didn't.
The lanes are filled with stork-news nonetheless,
White petals star-splayed, mimicking our village,
Whose spread arms pose as streets in our address.

Strange, changes. Now we're on a brand new railroad;
Vladivostok to Adriatic Sea;
At space-age white pavilions load and unload
One-car electric trains, infrequently.

Deaf

His girlfriend's gone, his heart is broken.
He lives on bread and knocks back beer.
He's thirty-nine and softly spoken.
He's glad of my impartial ear.

He curls up in his teenage bedroom,
Puts on a Crowded House cassette.
Nowhere to sit and little headroom.
He shows me photos of Tibet;

And souvenirs from Russia, Britain,
Indian gods and Afghan drums.
Books he's translated or co-written.
We turn to Islam. Morning comes.

His father fought for two world powers,
Survived two kinds of prison camp,
And farts away his final hours
In deaf neglect and rising damp.

Cape York

And I was in the middle of a muddy three-point turn
When in her blond contralto—no excitement or concern—
She asked me: "Can you drive a truck?" I said: "Well, I could learn."

All torrid week she'd puzzled me, my cousin in the cliffs,
With open-ended comments and provocative what ifs
And sniggering complaints about her husband and their tiffs.

And asking me—in front of him—"the dunny chain is broke.
I don't suppose you'd help me, love? I think it needs a bloke"—
Too much for me, the mummy's boy, the yuppie from up smoke.

Then, over home-made lemonade, the last day of my stay:
"I only keep Frank for his truck"—she smiled against the bay,
Which foamed beneath the mountains. And the sunshine
    blazed away;

And as I passed the outhouse on departing, there was Frank.
He'd fainted by the window, overlooking where we drank,
And swarming insects ate him, and his wounds already stank.

An hour later, driving home, I thought I'd phone ahead;
Picked up my mobile…realized I was phoning *her* instead.
I asked her: "How's he coming on?" "He's almost through," she said.

And I was in the middle of a muddy three-point turn
When in her blond contralto—no excitement or concern—
She asked me: "Can you drive a truck?" I said: "Well, I could learn."

Raumfahrt

How the imagination can wander!
I'm thinking of Immanuel Kant.
He believed in Martians.

He thought they were a lot cleverer than us.
They live further away from the sun, you see,
And we all know about those savages down
    near the Equator

And how the people are much more civilized
The nearer you get to the Polar regions.
He didn't get much sun himself, old Kant,

And Königsberg
Was the closest he ever got
To the Poles.

Clicks

For me it's a source of amusement, the cluster of clicks
As my left leg begins to unbend: the echoing crack
And the stretching noise as it reaches its fullest extent.
The ripping of linen noise, the snap of a gangster's knuckles,
The creak of a bridge under stress. It prises me out into chuckles.
I ease it out straight and I slowly maneuver it back.
I could do it for hours. Although you prefer me unbent
And simple to fix.
Slipped easily into each other's overcoat pockets, slim
And soft and together. No five years between us. Nothing
Worth more than a grimace or five midnight minutes discussing.
Though my trick with the clicks in my leg always makes
   you look grim,

For me it's a source of amusement. And a source of eternal despair
Are the breakable bones of your tiny white wrist
As your hand flops silently down to support your chin,
As you open a grin
Through your loosening hair,
Refuse to close the sheen of your eyes and refuse to be kissed.

The Translator

Between the hearts of Europe and of Asia,
Or halfway from São Paulo to New York,
I peddle my inherited aphasia
Wherever light is dim and footpaths fork.

A parasite on anything uncertain—
A medium for codifying fear—
A tiny bore-hole through an iron curtain—
My world is shrinking fast. Don't come too near.

Philology

These words are not my own. They flow unguided
Through lips and ears. They've mixed and interbred.
They've bombed around, and bruised where
   they've collided,
And changed their meaning each time they've been said.

Don't talk of their descent or evolution.
Don't group them into groups. Draw me no tree.
Don't tell me to protect them from pollution.
They're global. And they don't belong to me.

They rocket out the second that I breathe them.
They cloud the air and fumigate the phone.
I nourish and inherit and bequeath them.
They pass me by. These words are not my own.

Romeo and Juliet—Free Delivery

He never knew a finer hour, that priest!
It went like clockwork. We hopped on a bus—
Me and my girl (officially deceased)—
And fled to Mantua. Now look at us.
A pizzeria and three grown-up kids,
A few more lines, some extra pounds of flesh.
A marriage that has sometimes hit the skids,
A romance where at least the topping's fresh.
And if I had my time again—who knows?
Sometimes I wish fair Rosaline would call,
Or wish I'd had the courage to propose
To her. It took the madness of that ball
To loosen me—the night I met my wife.
I worry too much. Story of my life.

Reassessment

The last time that I saw her
(Over a year, it's been),
She was the loveliest creature
That I had ever seen.

But now we're re-united,
It really is quite strange.
She's nice, but nothing special.
Funny how people change.

Suburbiana

A housewife blooms in outskirt land, in garden-gnome suburbia,
In permanent bikini, in a baking landlocked scrub.
A town that could be anywhere from Swabia to Serbia;
The third street on the right from Jimi's Pub.

A long thin town that sheaths a road the Danube spills its silt on,
Replete with prefab hair salons and dancing-girl hotels;
Inside a house that's always growing, always being built on,
Black-haired and sea-green-eyed, this housewife dwells.

Beside the World War monument, along the topless corso,
Beneath the TV dishes bringing world and county news,
You kiss her tattooed biceps and her tanned and wiry torso,
You kiss her pink clear plastic high-heeled shoes.

The City

This is what the city is like.

A short lad of about sixteen
With the rasping, toneless voice of a seventy-year-old
Serenades a tube train full of people.
He seems to think
He's a good singer,
Shutting his eyes and swaying
And contorting his husky croak
Into prolonged vibratos.
It's an incredibly weird sound.
All the people wince and grit their teeth
As they do each time they see him.

But today there is added entertainment.
A little terrier someone has brought onto the train
Starts barking angrily at the singer.
He ignores it and carries on.
They make a strange duet.
A few smiles light up a few faces
In the dingy corridor they are all sat or stood along.
Everybody hated the sound that boy made
Though they were too polite to say so;
The dog's vehement disapproval
Puts the final stamp on it.

One man in late middle-age
Risks a broad grin.
He is unable to smile to himself
Or at some inanimate object.
His grin and eyes are turned first on the singer
And then on a number of his fellow-passengers.
He works along a line,
Seeking out smirks
That might break into grins to answer his own
When they catch his eye.
But each time he finds one,
It disappears,
Replaced by a look of abstraction or a frown.

On the Bottom Step

She sat me on the bottom step and sat herself beside,
She put her arms around me and she kissed me and she sighed,
And said as I looked into her lovely eyes of blue:
"You never will love me as much as I love you.

"For a woman's love is deeper than a man can comprehend.
You can lose yourself inside it, and never reach the end,
And find that you are drowning in my lovely eyes of blue."
She held me tight and sighed again, and I sighed too.

Needing Bridges

Each bridge defines a stretch of the flat town,
Lords over it, and makes its road continue
Deep into it; keeps taut its pulsing sinew—
But wartime photos show those bridges down,

And one ad-hoc bridge that was soon destroyed.
Plaques, pointing statues, tell the tale. It throws me.
I dream how this wet air might still enclose me,
Walking out on the flat face of that void...

The hilly town, sure in its bluff terrain,
Of course, has its own shape, is less in need.
This tram I'm in now, fastening the river,

That marbles with unnecessary rain,
Stanches the doubt. Up there we view, we read,
We live; a bridge would be how we deliver.

Gypsy

I'm telling the truth, not just being evasive:
I *don't* know you,
Although I do remember
When I met you before
And shook your hand as I do now
And smiled stupidly as I do now,
Thrilled and made nervous
By your black eyes and mocking voice.
Then, if memory serves, you were polite enough
To pour some sweet pink liqueur down my throat
Before asking for money
And pinching my hat
Which was when my spirit of fun
Failed me
And I grabbed it back and crossed the road.

Yes, I know you,
From the flash of your eyes and the curve of your lips
And the confidence of that "give me."
And I know your kind
And why the good folks say you're bad.
Because you have no guilt and no responsibility
And you're happy that way.
You could go through school and get a job,
And maybe I really could be your "friend,"
But why should you bother?
With your Gypsy friends
And that lilt in your voice
You have enough to survive,
And anyone not of your race
Is not to be loved
But to be cheated with the promise of love.

Knowing this,
I know all I need to know about you.
But I can't know as much as I want to know.
So I deny you and walk away,
Vaguely hoping we'll meet again.

Before Your Time

So here you are again,
Though older than back then.
Late night, a Camel Light,
Old jeans, and CNN.
It's kind of middle age;
Feels like the final page.
Just one of many men—
Here you are again.

Imagine you restart,
Act out the same old part.
Your eyes find no surprise
And nothing hurts your heart.
The night you spent with her—
The fight—they all recur.
Or would she not depart
If you could restart?

You're old before your time,
Not shocked by any crime.
Neat Scotch; the screen keeps watch,
And early church bells chime.
You know she'll never come,
And all you feel is numb.
You skate, you do not climb—
Old before your time.

Man and Boy

"Are you a man," she asked, "or just a boy?"
And pinned him to the corner of the bed.
"Well, that depends on what you'd most enjoy."
She kissed him gently. "You're a man," she said.

Handsome Shallow

Oh pity us, the handsome shallow people,
A much maligned and disadvantaged bunch.
The charming tailors' dummies
Who have perfect teeth and tummies
But who don't pour forth opinions over lunch.

It's no fun being beautiful but boring.
In love and in career we have no luck.
We make a good impression
At the pre-induction session
But we're ditched before we've earned a single buck.

For public taste prefers the smart but homely.
The hairy but articulate stand tall.
If trenchant observations
Don't infuse your conversations
Then the world's most shapely butt won't break your fall.

Aye, through the sentried palace of ambition
How fast the ugly know-it-all proceeds,
While we're kept at a distance
By a puritan insistence
On assessing people by their words and deeds!

Oh drop your guard, embrace the bland but pretty,
The perfect-bodied intellectual whelps.
We lack the mental power
Of a Kant or Schopenhauer
But we're always on for screwing, if that helps.

Yes, though we have to bear so much injustice,
We're not too hard to please, it must be said.
And so, if you've a mind to
Ease the lot we've been consigned to,
Then tonight, take someone cute but dull to bed.

First Impressions

I felt slightly self-conscious
Being introduced to him
While I was lying under a blanket with her
And leaning against a tree
On a roundabout island
Late at night
With a Dostoevsky novel in one hand
And a bottle of sweet Martini in the other.

I mean, he might have thought I was a bit eccentric,
Or something.

But I felt a bit better
When she explained
That this was the guy whose rough horseplay
Had caused the stuffing to come out
Of her much-esteemed cuddly crocodile.

Hurrah for our mutual friend,
One of life's free spirits,
Who freed our spirits too,
And without whose subversive influence
We might have met at some boring wine party
And talked about politics.

And Fall

A beautiful spring.
Sunny mornings with little snowflakes
And you with your easy shyness,
Your smiling melancholy.

The city rumbling through.
The party I threw the first warm week
When you made yourself the hostess;

Then half-hour phone calls
With half-minute silences,
Gently listening to each other's listen.

Sweet dreams, you said.
Your warm giggle. Your incredible eyes.
Our hands touching like children.

Losing sleep.
A slight apprehension
That spring and fall
Are the only seasons.

Welcome to Sarajevo

It's from *saraj*, the Turkish word for palace.
Any Turks here? We cater for all sorts.
One of the Empire's friendliest resorts,
This. The Miljacka valley brooks no malice.

Croat and Serb are summoned by soft bells
Of domed respective churches. The blue mosque
Of Husrev-beg welcomes both Gheg and Tosk.
This is Franz-Josef-Strasse. Good hotels.

And this is the bazaar. Don't get ripped off.
This Persian carpet going for a tenner,
I'm damned if that's come further than Vienna!

Don't miss the dervishes. Herr Al-Safavid
Serves Pilsner and strong coffee at the Hoff.
The synagogue's my hang-out. Ask for Dávid.

Baikal

We thought we'd discovered the sea, but the water was sweet,
And piercing white mist rolled away from the opposite shore.
Baikal, said the orange-faced natives. A hundred or more
Miles deep, we supposed. So we trampled a primitive street

And stayed a few months. It was wild. You could just see our feet
When we dived in the snow. We threw snowballs the size of a door.
We gave little local girls kvass and then gave them what for.
We drank the white air. Crouched around in soiled greatcoats to eat.

We had some adventures back then! Stamping down
    each new camp—
Tomsk, Bratsk, Olekminsk, Zashiversk—town by town we impressed
Our Slavic on tribesmen who quickly gave in and made friends;

And as this cold life and expansionist century ends,
Our sons build a Burg on the sea-bogs: their rare letters damp
With action. Out there where the action was always. The west.

Namely

The more I say your name, when people need it,
The more I have to ask it down the phone,
The more I hear or read it,
Implore or soothe or plead it,
The less it keeps me warm when I'm alone.

Heron's Nest

We're in some godforsaken Swabian village
That's reached by several train trips and a bus.
Beyond the stain of Stuttgart's urban spillage;
Where vineyards thin and forests brood: that's us.

And what I like is how the jaded schoolkids
Who live among these big-bad-wolf black woods
Flounce off the bus, pan-European cool kids,
With cracking gum, flicked hair, designer goods.

The town you catch that bus from has whole lanes full
Of fairy-story carpenters and smiths,
And one McDonald's. Hell, why pump your veins full
With dumplings and those marzipanny myths?

The Crush

I didn't know this, but apparently
Prokofiev died on the same day as Stalin.
His widow spent that weekend in and out
Of every florist in the Yellow Pages.
Sold out, my dear. Closed down. Gone out of business.
Uncomprehending phantoms packed the streets.
Trainloads of peasants! Lorryloads of roses!
Innocent people perished in the crush.

You didn't know this, but when you went mad
Because I let you leave after the ballet
Without the flowers that I'd given you,
And when we turned and walked, on your insistence,
All the way back, still arm in arm, to get them,
Uncomprehending phantoms packed the streets.
You my dictator! Me your sad musician!
Innocent people perished in the crush.

Elton Jim

At last I've worked out why
There's been this wildfire rumor
Amongst the folks at work that I
Have got a sense of humor.

With me you get the total man.
The funniness is not the plan.
That power is residual.
You want to laugh then laugh you can.
My current boss proclaims me "an
Amazing individual."

Got up. Plugged in my microphone.
Adjusted my recording levels.
Laid down a tinny keyboard drone,
Cranked up my rich bass-baritone,
Unleashed my inner devils.

No label—I suspect you sensed it.
I've no idea for who or what I sing.
A demo needn't be for anything.
It could just be against it.

Got up, de-tuned guitar, and played
Another song, more mellow, faster.
Wiped off the input jacks, and made
A master.

At last I think I see—
The truth could not be plainer—
Why folks at work conceive of me
As just an entertainer.

Irresolution

This New Year's, I wasn't invited to anyone's house.
I didn't go angling for invites, so that's no surprise.
I stood on my balcony watching the street shooting off.
I'm nursing the cold I contract every time I stop work.

I've worked on two letters to you in the course of the day—
Please give me just one final chance and Goodbye it's been fun.
It only seems apt to be looking both forward and back.
My parents phoned up and they both recommended fresh fruit.

Last New Year's, a girl who was doing her best to get fresh
Said if I was lonely that night I'd be lonely all year.
I left unobserved about two and I thought about you.
I still don't know whether or not her prediction came true.

Anecdote

Despite being communists,
The leaders of Romania
Between World War Two and 1989
Were also nationalists.

Towns which had always
Borne Hungarian or German names
Were officially rebaptized
With Romanian ones.

My parents' village slipped through the net
And kept the same name
Throughout those atheist days.
Gottlob. Praise God.

Resort

We waited for the public bus one hour
(The private ones are frequent, but cost more),
And used this time to slander those in power
And reaffirm how righteous are the poor.

The thermal pools were packed on our arrival—
So many fools prepared to pay that price!
Then, since we'd brought some cake to aid survival,
We crouched beside a bar and shared one slice.

We would have loved to sip a Segafredo,
Regaled by many a disco-beat CD;
Instead, we hiked up to our usual meadow:
A-strewn with stinking litter, true, but free.

There, half-undressed, and turning deep vermilion,
Lulled by the tolling of a sleepy kirk,
We talked of soaps Peruvian and Chilean
And cursed this wretched life of endless work.

Lying Still

After a few nights of
Going to sleep in the searing heat
Drunk on fine fruit spirits,
I found my sheets took on a strange smell:

A headier, purer,
Double-distilled potion filled my sweat.
Soon I'll be fermenting,
Be a reaction, be truly still.

Find a Spot

The teacher bellows "Find a spot!"—your skinny arms shoot out—
You fan off from your fellows and you start to spin about,
And once or twice you give your friend an accidental clout;

You move a little to the right, a little further back,
Until you're out of danger from an accidental whack;
The piano starts, you take deep breaths, your body goes all slack;

You don't know if you're at the beach or if you're still at school,
You move the way the music moves, you don't care if it's cool,
You do your thing, you don't hurt others, that's the only rule;

But sometimes it takes thirty years—and that's a long long hike—
To earn enough to live on from a job you don't dislike,
And still have time at weekends to play drums or ride your bike,

And build your kind of home—you may get married, you may not.
And some folks say they've lost their way. It bothers them a lot.
Relax. It's not the place you're in. It's if you find a spot.

About The Author

David Hill is a writer, translator, and editor.

Covering economy, travel and culture, he has contributed to nonfiction books published by Blue Guides, Oxford Business Group, and the Stockholm Network, and to news products from the *Financial Times* and *Economist* groups. He was editor-in-chief of the *Budapest Business Journal* in 2004-05.

As a literary writer, he has been published in anthologies from Rattapallax (US), Bluechrome (UK) and DC Books (Canada). A debut collection of poetry was issued in 1999 by the UK's National Poetry Foundation. His literary translations have appeared in *The Independent* and the *Times Literary Supplement*.

He has provided lyrics for recording artists, including the Little Cow band. Commissions for stage and screen include a version of Molière's *Misanthrope*. He has spoken at conferences, festivals, comedy shows, and arts events in Seattle, New York, London, Amsterdam, Copenhagen, Vienna, Budapest, and Prague.

David Hill studied languages at Oxford University, graduating with a First in 1995. He lives with his wife in the northwest United States. His website is www.davidhill.biz.

2113145